PORTER'S BAR B Q

LaVonne Rice
La Vonne Rice
started Porters Woodsmoke
Bar.B-Q five years ago
— and doing real well.

HAMBURGER MARY'S

HAMBURGER MARY'S

rock·roll fashions

SPOT TAVERN

Sunday Morning.

ARGUS BISTRO

Gertrude →
a mean mean
bull bitch

LAYOUT

Barbara Hahn, Portland, Oregon

COLOR SEPARATIONS

Spectrum West Inc., Beaverton, Oregon

PRINTER

Millcross Lithography, Portland, Oregon

BOOKBINDER

Lincoln & Allen, Portland, Oregon

ISBN 0-9644651-0-8

Published by Chetwynd Stapylton Inc.

Copyright ©1994 by William Papas

Manufactured in the United States of America.

This book is dedicated to Gertrude, our eccentric spotted hound, who used to arrive each morning at the door of our first apartment to depart promptly at five. We assumed she was a latchkey dog, thankful to have company during the day, so it was with some embarrassment when, six months later, her rightful owner made contact with us and we learned that he, too, worked at home. A sensible man, he accepted that she preferred our company and before he moved to Puerto Rico he gave her to us. She has given us much joy, and some pain, while accompanying us on so many forays around the city of Portland over the past ten years.

"Gertrude" named after One of Tessa's aloof Aunts
Best Friends. Alaska, Tennessee, Washington, Alabama, Monty & Maggie.
Height 27" Length 57" Weight 102½ lbs. Age 15.

GOOD CITIZENS ARE
THE RICHES OF A CITY

4

The Skidmore Fountain

River place.

5

"J.E. Bud Clark"

"I need a lot of Pockets for
scarves, hats, gloves, Mail
Organizer Computors and..."

6

"Good citizens are the riches of a city", an inscription on the Skidmore Fountain, has never been truer with the arrival of Bill and Tessa Papas to Portland. Bill and Tessa are citizens of the planet who have made Portland their family home becoming one of Portland's greatest riches as this book demonstrates.

Bill with his quick eye and the swirling magic of his pen brings to life the Portland streets populated with its riches, the good citizens and visitors of the city. The people of Portland have worked hard to plan, create and maintain a vibrant inner city and downtown. Bill lets you have a glimpse of that vibrancy through his eyes.

Tessa puts it into the written word, expanding with history and anecdote to give you the background on their views of Portland and its story. It is a young city with a desire to retain and expand its livability. *Papas' Portland* might even open some Portlanders' eyes to the very wonderful place where they live.

I love the City of Portland and all its good citizens. *Papas' Portland* will help you to love Portland as I do and a little bit more.

Bud Clark

Bud on his
Bike FRIDAY
(a fold up bike –
fits into a Suitcase

7

Text by Tessa Papas
Drawings & paintings by Bill Papas

Papas'
PORTLAND

Looking at Downtown Portland from the East Side.

PORTLAND'S HISTORY

A lawyer and a drifter were the founding fathers. In 1843 while voyaging by canoe from Fort Vancouver to Oregon City, the capital of the Oregon Territory, they stopped at "the clearing", an Indian resting place on the west bank of the Willamette. It was the drifter, William Overton, who suggested to the lawyer, Asa Lovejoy late of Boston, that this would be a good place to stake a claim to the 640 free acres that were offered to pioneers on the assumption that Oregon would soon become a U.S. Territory. The feckless Overton did not have the required 25¢ filing fee so Lovejoy paid and in return was given half of Overton's claim; 320 acres that would become the center of downtown Portland. Overton did not stay around his city long but, before he left never to be seen again, he bartered the other half of his claim to Francis Pettygrove, a New Englander like Lovejoy. The two men decided to toss a coin for the name of their new city. Pettygrove, from Portland, Maine, won and Portland became Portland.

Other pioneers filed claims. Among them, a Captain John Couch, who decided that Portland was the ideal deep water port that he had been seeking on the West Coast and a Daniel Lownsdale who set up a tannery, the first west of the Rockies, on what is now Civic Stadium. Thanks to Captain Couch Portland now had a deep water port while Lownsdale's contribution was to build an all weather planked road through a canyon in the West Hills that gave access to the rich farmlands of the Tualatin Valley. Then gold was discovered in California in 1848. This was the boost that the city needed to catapult it from frontier town to fledgling metropolis. The reason was lumber. A thousand board feet that cost $30 in Oregon could be sold in San Francisco for $1,350. The city was incorporated in 1851, churches and a jail were built, a city planning board formed (one of their first actions was to set aside twenty five contiguous city blocks for parks) and the *Oregonian* started publication under the editorship of Thomas Dryer. By 1858 the population was 2,000, there were over a hundred shops and the city's first school had been built on what is now Pioneer Courthouse Square. Oregon officially became a state that year, but Portlanders were far more excited about the first ascent of Mt. Hood than the news they were now part of the Union. Another gold rush boom in the 1860's, this time in Eastern Oregon and Idaho, saw a dramatic increase in population and in the look of the city. The tree stumps that had earned Portland the unflattering title of "Stumptown" were finally pulled out. Large houses with large gardens were built and more trees and parks planted. A six miles an hour speed limit in residential areas was enforced, dogs without collars were impounded, and the city took on the sobriquet of "a city of homes", a description that applies as much today as it did then. The Historical Society was formed and the public library was built during this time. The transcontinental railway line reached Portland with much fanfare in 1883. City Hall was built ten years later, the first art museum and art school on the west coast soon followed. The crown jewel of the city, the chateau-like Portland Hotel, was completed in 1890.

Portland's Golden Age started with the turn of the century and lasted until after the end of World War I. The new age kicked off with a World Fair to celebrate the centenary of Lewis and Clark. The city fathers had become worried that upstart Seattle was

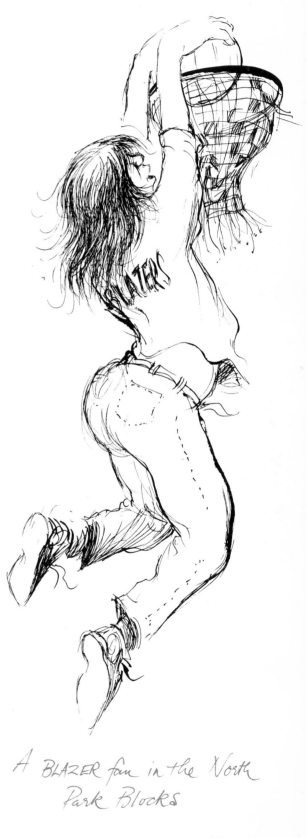

A BLAZER fan in the North Park Blocks

11

outstripping Portland in size and importance so they decided a world class fair would put the city on the map. Frederick Law Olmsted, the designer of New York's Central Park, was asked to plan the fair around a large lake in Northwest Portland. President Roosevelt opened it via telegraph. Fourteen countries were represented and nearly 3 million people visited to gawk at the pavilions, the rose gardens and the latest technological miracle, thousands of electric lights. Interestingly the foreign exhibitor with the largest pavilion was Japan, a portent that the state's future trading focus would be with the Pacific Rim. Portland became a familiar word around the country and the fair succeeded as the city elders had hoped. The population jumped from 90,000 to 250,000 by 1910. The economy boomed. Portland's first skyscraper, a daring twelve stories high, was built. Hundreds of streetcars crossed the Willamette's four bridges and provided inexpensive and effective mass transport. Meier & Frank and Lipman Wolfe department stores opened, building continued apace and Portland's society enjoyed itself with garden clubs, hunt clubs, rugby, cricket, golf and croquet games and balls and cotillions at the Portland Hotel. The intelligentsia delighted in the founding of Reed College with its emphasis on scholastic ability, an emphasis that has made Reed one of the foremost liberal arts colleges in the country today. They took part in the Sunday Forum Discussion Club formed by C.E.S. Wood and Rabbi Stephen Wise, read the literary magazine *Pacific Monthly*, forerunner of *Sunset Magazine,* and attended the many theaters and the opera. Physical health was just as well cared for as the intellectual. Portland boasted some of the finest medical care on the west coast with the founding of the Good Samaritan Hospital in 1875. The city had the reputation as one of the healthiest places in the USA, due not only to its medical care but also to the temperate climate and the clean water of the Bull Run reservoir, the same water that runs through the city's faucets today.

There was of course a dark side to this idyllic life. Since the first boom in the 1850's, saloons, gambling houses and brothels had been built near the port in what is now Old Town to provide entertainment for the sailors and drifters. Chinese opium dens abounded and underneath Old Town was a warren of tunnels. Many an unfortunate awoke from a drunken stupor to find that he had been shanghaied. A tale is told of one sea captain, desperate for a crew, accepting twenty unconscious men. As he crossed the Columbia bar the next morning he discovered that his crew was not merely unconscious, they were all dead. His procurer, unable to find anyone in the bars, had raided the nearest mortuary.

By 1912 there were at least 400 "immoral places". A report published the same year revealed so much vice and corruption that the city was forced to do something about it. An ordinance named the "tin plate law" was passed. Any building that housed a brothel or a short-term hotel was required to have the owner's name posted. The idea was to shame the landlords into closing their lucrative rentals and, as many of the buildings were owned by the same upright burghers who were making so much fuss about crime, it might have been an embarrassing situation. However the law failed to mention that the plaques had to be in English and as few citizens could read Urdu, Sanskrit or Hebrew no one learned who the landlords actually were.

The effects of the Depression were slow to reach Portland. Its businessmen in general were not speculators, but by the mid thirties Governor Meier had declared the state bankrupt. In 1929 downtown Portland cut itself off from the river by destroying the wharves and building a seawall. With the advent of the automobile more and more people moved out to the new suburbs and by the early 40's the city was a shabby, dispirited place. Two events brought it out of its stupor. One was the building of the Bonneville Dam in 1937, which provided jobs and a constant source of cheap power, and the other was America's embroilment in World War II. Ships had to be built and Portland's shipyards were put into overdrive. Over 100,000 workers descended on the city, a large number of them blacks from the South. This boom also provided work for women. 20,000 were employed by the Kaiser shipyards alone and many, as more and more men were called up, became electricians, painters and welders earning the same as their male counterparts, an impressive $1.20 an hour.

In Line Skaters in Tom McCall Park

During the 50's Portland voters consistently turned down any ballot measure to improve the city. More and more businesses moved away and by 1960 the number of people coming downtown to shop or go to a movie had dropped by a third. The population within the city's limits had also decreased. This was to be compared with Seattle which had grown 30% over the same period. The first step to improve downtown was taken when the newly formed Development Commission was given a federal grant to raze fifty four blocks of old neighborhoods in South Portland. The urban renewal plan called for new office towers and high rise apartment buildings, the Civic Auditorium, parks, gardens and fountains. At the same time Portland State College was moved to the south end of the Park Blocks and Lloyd Center, just across the Willamette on the east side, was built. It had the distinction of being the largest mall at that time in the USA.

In 1937 Lewis Mumford, the famous urban planner, said during a visit to Portland, "In providing for new developments you have an opportunity here to do a job of city planning like nowhere else in the world". But it was not until the early 70's that a comprehensive city plan was implemented. The young mayor of Portland, Neil Goldschmidt, and his board of Commissioners were mostly responsible for the Downtown Plan. Under their guidance public agencies were formed like Tri-Met, Metro and a new Port of Portland agency. The old expressway that ran along the Willamette was torn up and Waterfront Park, later Tom McCall Park, put in its place. The Central City Plan has been stringently adhered to and today one can see the fruits of this planning effort. In the decade that Bill and I have lived in Portland we have seen the city, unlike most American cities, improve each year. We have seen the opening of Pioneer Courthouse Square, the completion of the eastside light rail and the start of the west, the building of RiverPlace, of Pioneer Mall, of the Performing Arts Center, and the transformation of the Pearl District. Above all we have watched the city come alive with people; people thronging the sidewalks day and night, week day or weekend, people relaxing, strolling, exercising, fishing, shopping, sidewalk café sitting and people living in the new lofts, apartments, condominiums and townhouses that have been built all over downtown. Ten years ago, in Geneva, we met a journalist who had just had an article published in Harpers. He had been asked to name the ten most livable cities in the world and Portland was the only North American city he had selected. His was the first of an ever increasing number of accolades that claim we live in "America's most livable city."

"Maggie" named after Margaret Thatcher.
— Gertrudes best friend.
Height 6¼" Length 11¾" weight 4⅞ lb.

looking North from Atwaters.

Mt Rainier
Highest point in Washington
Elevation - 14,408ft
Distance - 102 Miles

Mt St. Helens
Elevation 8,363 ft.
Distance - 50 miles

Mt Adams.
Elevation - 12,307 ft
Distance - 74 miles

Mt Hood
Highest point in Oregon
Elevation - 11,245 ft.
Distance - 50 miles

THE RIVER

Portland has also been described as "a city that gravity built". Due to its situation on the Willamette with easy access to the Columbia, Captain Couch was able to persuade other sea captains that Portland was an excellent port despite the 87 mile journey upriver from the Pacific Ocean. It was fortuitous that gold was discovered in California in the 1840's because it enabled Portland to become a major supplier of lumber and wheat. By 1849 at least twenty ships a day were readied at the Stark Street wharves for the voyage to San Francisco. At about the same time, the *Sally Brown* sailed for Liverpool in England with a load of wheat, the first harbinger that Portland would become the largest wheat shipping port of the USA. Today the port is full of grain ships from Russia, China and Europe carrying the same wheat that was in the *Sally Brown's* hold. It is still barged down the Columbia from eastern Washington and Oregon to Portland's silos that line the river's banks north of the Steel Bridge. In the 1860's gold was discovered in Idaho and a former Mississippi riverboat captain, named John Ainsworth, formed the Oregon Steam Navigation Company. This company, based in Portland, had the monopoly on all travel by river to the "Inland Empire" as it was termed. With the advent of the railroads passenger travel on the river declined but as a working port Portland slowly increased in importance. The docks and terminals expanded downriver to the confluence of the Willamette and Columbia rivers. During World War II Portland's ship-building industry boomed. Over 100,000 workers descended on Swan Island to jobs at the Kaiser Shipyards. At the peak of the boom the yards were churning out a completed Liberty ship every eleven days. Today, thousands of cars from Japan and Korea are landed at the port for distribution throughout the country. Wheat and timber shipments and the ship repair drydocks have combined to make Portland the third largest port on the west coast. While the industrial nature of the Willamette continued unabated, the recreational side was sorely neglected. It was not until the 1970's, thanks to the vision of the then mayor, Neil Goldschmidt, and the Governor, Tom McCall, that an expressway that ran alongside the river was ripped out and Riverfront Park, now Tom McCall Park was put in its place. Pollution was curbed, salmon returned and today it is not uncommon to see a businessman in suit and tie fishing for a spring chinook during his lunch break. In summer the river hums with watersport activity; water skiers, sail boats, noisy jet skis and even swimmers. House-boats moored at Sellwood and the south end of Ross Island are fashionable neighborhoods. Passenger travel on the river has returned with a spate of tour boats, among them two sternwheelers reminiscent of the heyday of the Oregon Steam Navigation Company.

BRIDGES

An out of town friend, on seeing downtown for the first time from the east bank freeway, commented that Portland reminded her of a more intimate London where she had lived for many years. "The bridges are as varied but the setting is prettier", she said. I concur. The bridges have earned Portland the epithet of Bridgetown. But for the first forty years of the city's history there were none. Portland was settled on the west bank and for a long time the east bank remained farm land and wilderness with access only by the Stark Street Ferry. However in 1887, the first version of the Morrison Bridge was built followed by the Steel Bridge, the first bridge built of steel on the west coast. Almost immediately the whole complexion of east Portland changed. The farms rapidly gave way to new subdivisions such as Irvington, Eastmoreland and Ladd's Addition. More bridges were built, newly electrified trolleys crossed the bridges to the new suburbs and East Portland became boom town. Lots were sold and houses were built. One developer boasted that no house in his development could cost under $2,000 thus, he said, assuring the surroundings, and some of Portland's biggest fortunes were made in real estate. Today there are eight bridges across the Willamette in the downtown area. The Morrison, Steel and Hawthorne bridges have been rebuilt three times, the Burnside twice. The two most recent are the Marquam, which carries freeway traffic across the southern end of the city, and the Fremont which does the same for the northern end. The Fremont was constructed in one piece down river at St. Helens and then barged to its site where two large helicopters guided it into position. The red Broadway Bridge is the longest drawbridge in Portland. When it opened in 1912 there were just 2,500 registered vehicles in the city, but it was felt that the numbers might grow. How right! Three years later there were 14,000 registered vehicles and Portland was experiencing its first traffic jams. Today the bridge provides a roosting place

Willamette
River
Portland
Papas 1993

麦沅健
Mak Yuen Kin
Waitress at.

ROBERT (BOB) LOUIE   GROCERY: 223-1777
                      223-1222
                      RESTAURANT
                      220-0235

WHOLESALE
and RETAIL
CHINESE and   301 N.W. 4TH AVE.
ORIENTAL   PORTLAND, OR 97209
GROCERIES

FOOD
TO GO
DIM SUM
CHINESE FOOD
SPECIALTY

for thousands of birds that swirl in at dusk and, should one be stuck in a traffic jam, a venue to admire the newly restored advertisements that adorn Albers Mill. In 1989 Hugh Boatright, a self taught artist, could be seen working on the murals. Bill Naito, the developer of Albers Mill, had seen his work in a downtown bar and asked him to repaint the old advertisements. After a street kid said that he would no longer spray the mill with graffiti because the restoration was too beautiful to spoil, Hugh commented, "If my work makes people happy then I feel I've done something worthwhile; what more can you ask out of life if you're an artist?"

The Hawthorne Bridge provides a backdrop to Salmon Springs, Gertrude's favorite fountain. On a hot day it is crowded with shrieking children who play in and under the jets and laugh at Gertrude as she tries to bite the water.

Hugh Boatright relaxing during Mural Painting.

Salmon Street Spring
Gov Tom McCall Waterfront Park
Portland OR 1989

Salmon Springs on a Sunny Day!

REMOTE CONTROL

ANDY ADDAMS

changes every so —

Fun to watch Tom

Porcupine Spike

River Place — Portland
Papas 1993

RIVERPLACE & WATERFRONT PARK

To get an idea of how much Portland has changed over the past ten years, it is interesting to walk from RiverPlace to the Japanese Garden north of the Burnside Bridge. In 1984, when Bill and I first arrived in Portland, RiverPlace was a bare riverbank. But then, almost overnight, a series of pastel clapboard condominiums appeared, punctuated at one end by the floating Newport Bay restaurant, and at the other by the turreted RiverPlace Hotel with the city's most popular marina in the middle. On a warm summer weekend the esplanade is a danger zone of in-line skaters, cyclists, and joggers weaving their way between the more sedentary boutique strollers and restaurant sitters. Soon the esplanade will extend southward towards John Landing through more condominiums, shops and offices.

Pre-1974, the waterfront was a disaster zone. An expressway ran along the west bank, cutting access to the river. Not that there was much reason to visit it - its banks were rat infested and its water filthy. But 1974 saw the ripping out of the expressway and the creation of the park with its acres of grass, trees, an embankment and promenade. The park plays host to an ever increasing number of celebrations. Cinco de Mayo in May, the Bite and the Beer festivals later in summer, concerts of all shades of music in between, and the Fun Center of June's Rose Festival are all centered on the banks of the Willamette. A precursor of the Rose Festival took place in the late 1890's. The rose had been adopted as Portland's symbol and roses were planted all over the city. A group of women who called themselves the Mystic Order of the Rose gave away free cuttings and the Order of the Royal Rosarians was formed. In their white suits and boaters, they are still an integral part of the parade. The first Rose Festival proper took place in 1907. The program read "Monster parade of Floral Decorated Automobiles, Competitive

Floats, Equestrian Clubs, Military and Bands ...." The first Queen Flora was the daughter of the Governor of Oregon. Little has changed since. The Festival now extends over three weeks instead of three days. There are more parades, an airshow, Indy races, naval ships docking at the seawall and of course, the Fun Center down at the waterfront. Hundreds of thousands ride the Big Wheels that tower above the trees and, as it usually rains, they slosh around in the mud gawking at the ships and feasting on Elephant Ears and other calorific delights. I am always surprised at how quickly the grass recuperates from these regular onslaughts.

Fishermen on the Waterfront. Catching Fish!

Rose Festival—with the Fleet in Town

SATURDAY MARKET

Further north is the Saturday Market. It opened twenty odd years ago under the Burnside Bridge in an area that was still part of Skid Row. It was considered quite daring to venture to the market back then, but times change, and now it is crammed with shoppers and tourists every Saturday and Sunday from April until Christmas. In fact it has been so successful, that the booths have expanded across Ankeny Plaza and into the courtyard of the New Market Theater. A venue for Oregon craftsmen, and, it seems, every aging hippie north of Berkeley, the many booths display anything and everything providing it is made by hand. On a recent visit I found Whirly Bird Spinners, handmade basic survival tools, pine needle basketry and painted antique roofing signs among the more mundane pottery, wooden boxes and jewelry. I was pleased to see that the Spoonman was still around. Ten years ago I had bought one of his "Knife through the Head" hats for a nephew, a most popular Christmas present. On the same aisle I met Julie who has had a booth here for fifteen years. She sells leather belts and wallets that she makes at her home in Hillsboro. The Saturday Market is her only outlet and she remembers the first years. "Then, $150 a day was a fortune. Today I cry if I only make a $150 in a day!" She says the leather she uses has doubled in cost but her prices are not that much higher than when she started. I have to admit that twenty dollars for a handmade leather belt and buckle is quite a bargain. In the center of the Market is the Food Court where most ethnic food cravings can be satisfied. There are Indian curries, Middle Eastern shish kebabs, sambusas from Ethiopia, Chinese, Thai and Vietnamese noodles, Southern ribs and even Cornish pasties and sausage rolls made and sold by an Englishman from Liverpool. Limeys is owned by Ray who has lived here fourteen years. He loves Portland, he says, more than Liverpool, London or even Amsterdam where he lived for a time.

The Skidmore Fountain serves as a meeting place, though in fact it's specified use was not only for humans but for horses and dogs as well. Stephen Skidmore was a city commissioner who went to the Paris Exposition of 1878 and was so impressed by the European fountains that he left a bequest in his will for one to be built in Portland. The fountain was erected in 1888 and became the immediate pride of the city. Over the years it fell into disrepair, the area became part of Skid

Row and the horses that drank from it were replaced by automobiles. It was not until the 1980's when Old Town enjoyed a renaissance that the fountain regained prominence and usefulness. Today police horses and at least one dog I know drink from its waters. The saying on its base is much quoted, "Good citizens are the riches of a city". The city in question was Athens in 400 BC but it is just as apt for today's Portland.

The courtyard of the New Market Theater is also crowded with Market booths. In 1872, the city fathers decided that Portland needed a theater. So architects Piper and Burton designed an elaborate and grandiose building replete with a large stage and a 40 by 60-foot drop curtain. However, the actors and singers were confined to the upper two floors because at ground level there were farmers, butchers and grocers selling their produce from the twenty eight marble counters that comprised the market part of the building. Outside of Covent Garden in London, one wonders how many other cities have successfully combined produce and opera! The New Market Theater still stands. It is well restored and it can be said that the old tradition continues; food stalls abound and impromptu concerts are the norm!

Good Time
Rock & Roll
Theo. born
& brought up
in Portland

THEO
GOOD TIME

30

JAPANESE-AMERICAN HISTORICAL PLAZA

North of the Burnside Bridge is the Japanese-American Historical Plaza. It is a reflective place of almond trees, stones and two rock pillars inscribed with poetry to commemorate the lives of the *Issei,* Japanese pioneers many of whom were later interned during World War II. Opposite the park is a warehouse whose most noticeable feature is a neon reindeer, symbol of White Stag Sportswear, on its roof. One enters the warehouse by way of a nondescript door and mounts an equally unimpressive set of stairs into a large open loft whose only apparent concession to the modern world is a number of computers. This is the domain of a man and his family who have had an immeasurable

Bill Naito

effect on the preservation and restoration of many of Portland's old buildings, particularly the cast iron beauties on First and Second Avenues in Old Town. Bill Naito sits behind a large desk chewing on an unlit cigar. He tells us that his father came from Japan in 1916 and worked as a houseboy for the Lipman family, owners of one of Portland's first department stores. One of the things that impressed the young immigrant most was the turkey dinner that was served each Sunday. Naito senior was obviously a man of ambition and, by the 1930's, had learned English and opened an accounting office on SW 10th Avenue. One of the real estate deals that has given Bill great satisfaction was to buy and convert the old Lipman Wolfe department store into the Galleria. It is exactly opposite his father's old office. Bill is in his late 60's and still fired with ideas. He would like more recognition of the role that minorities have played in the development of Portland. The Chinese, he says have their Gate into Old Town on NW 4th. He envisions a Torii Gateway for the Japanese on NW 2nd and some Corinthian Pillars to honor the Greek community on NW 6th. He might have been pulling our legs but without a doubt minorities have not been particularly well treated throughout Oregon and Portland's history. Founded as it was by white New Englanders, there has been a prevailing sense that only the "right sort" should be allowed to share what was perceived as Eden. An early pioneer expressed relief that most of the local Indians had been wiped out by a mysterious disease, probably malaria, and that there was no need to indulge in ethnic cleansing, to use today's terminology. The first articles of the State Constitution forbade Negroes from living here and for a long time there were laws that forbade minorities from owning property in certain choice neighborhoods like the West Hills. During World War I people of German ancestry were not permitted within 300 yards of the Willamette. The Japanese were treated much worse during World War II; they were not allowed within three hundred miles of the Oregon coast and most ended up in detention camps in Idaho and Utah. On the other hand, from the beginning, there were always people who fought against such injustices and many of them have been or are being righted.

Before we leave Bill asks if we would like an ouzo. On hearing that we'd prefer bourbon, he reaches under his desk and produces an unopened bottle of Jack Daniels, explaining, somewhat sheepishly, that it was his birthday recently. We drink a toast to the future gateways.

FARMERS' MARKET

Another of Bill Naito's restorations, Albers Mill, overlooks the Farmers' Market that takes place every Saturday from Spring until Fall. It is an organic food lover's Paradise. Most of the vegetables are grown on Sauvie Island, another of Portland's delights. Less than half an hour from downtown, the island is a bucolic oasis of small farms, narrow winding roads, lakes, wildlife sanctuaries and the somewhat incongruous views of ships' superstructure rising above the trees as they ply the Ship canal.

Arden & Lilian Benson.
Selling Portland's Farmers Market T. Shirts

34

River Queen

Saturday Farmers Market

Gmapelli

Bill Herbert   John Linge.

Harold Unkeles

Steve Davis

Liz Mapelli at the top. &
the Boys from Carton Services.
—— bottom !!

Papas.

PEARL DISTRICT

Southwest of the Farmers' Market, past the police horses' stabling, is the Pearl District. In 1985 while looking for a large studio we stumbled on the Hoyt Street Loft Building, a dilapidated warehouse owned by five young men. We moved into 3000 square feet on the top story and could not believe the luxury of so much space! Other luxuries like heating were not available. So thanks to two large kerosene space heaters, we played host to the other tenants most winter afternoons. There was Liz Mapelli, a successful fused glass artist with installations all over the country, whose studio was in the basement. Her daughter, Sara, was Bill's assistant and she would arrive after school each day to help him print or paint. Her head was shaven except for a bright red or green topknot. I remember Liz remarking that if this was Sara's only form of teenage rebellion she was a lucky woman. Luckily it was. There was Hiroshi, a fashion photographer, who shared the top floor with us. He had no heating and I remember lines of shivering models in cheerleading outfits waiting to be photographed for some catalogue. There was Thomas Augustine who had one of the first galleries in the area and the distinction of naming the district. "We are the pearls," he said, "inside these rough and ugly exteriors!" At that time there were maybe three galleries and possibly two hundred artists intermingled

725 FLANDERS AND 8th Ave

with the traditional light industry of the district. A freight train still came down 13th Avenue past the boys of the Carton Service who would hurl rude epithets at Bill whenever he looked out of the studio windows. Today 13th Avenue is paved and the Carton Service has moved, their building bought for future loft living. Many of the old warehouses have been turned into lofts. The forty acres of Burlington Northern railyards are being developed and more than a thousand people are expected to move into the area. The central city plan called for growth north of Burnside. Once the Portland Development Commission bought Union Station and its surrounding acreage in 1988, change was inevitable. One looks back with a certain amount of nostalgia to those first years of the Pearl District. As Liz Mapelli remarked, we all had more time for each other then, but in balance, it is exciting to be part of such a massive expansion of the city.

Thomas Paul Augustine

Professor Extraodinaire
Art Critic Extraodinaire
Cultural Dilettante
Head Cognoscente

The dream of Henry Villard, a German immigrant who made his fortune in railroads, Union Station was supposed to be the grandest station west of the Mississippi. The designers of Pennsylvania Station in New York were hired but before the station was completed Mr. Villard went bankrupt. It was not until Jay Gould took over Villard's Union Pacific Railroad that a much less impressive station was completed in 1896. The station's heyday was in 1944 when 4.8 million people passed through its doors, but then it slowly sank into disrepair and little use. However, 1985 saw the relighting of its two famous neon signs, "Go by Train" and "Union Station". Portland Development Commission oversaw an extensive renovation and the opening of offices on the station's upper levels. The Greyhound Bus Station was relocated nearby and the extension of the Transit Malls from downtown was completed in 1994. There is talk of a Railway Museum and more housing on the vacant acreage. There is even a resurgence of train travel with lines of people waiting to ride the "Bullet" train on loan from Spain. If the plans for a high speed train corridor from Eugene to Vancouver BC come to fruition, Union Station's renaissance will be complete. The Portland Development Commission has played a major role in many projects in this part of town. At the turn of the century the North Park Blocks were used for picnics and recreation by the poorer families. There were tennis courts, lawns and a bandstand but as Old Town deteriorated the park became an outdoor dormitory and toilet. When we moved to our gallery in 1988, the park in front of us was a sea of bodies, drug dealers and prostitutes. Today, thanks to an investment of a couple of million dollars, the Park Blocks have returned to their original recreational intent. There are paths through some of the finest elms left in the city and new park benches on which to contemplate them, a fenced off children's playground, basketball courts and horseshoe pits in front of the gallery. A couple of years ago

Heinz Theil

Heinz Theil — old time friend.
Borrowed $4.25 every Monday
+ paid it back on Friday.
Then Catastrophy Struck
he came into $8,000 !!

we watched with surprise as a large fire engine drew up, its crew off loaded and a noisy game of horseshoes started. As one crew member explained, it was a quiet day for fires!

Another focus of the city has been to invest in the SRO program. Old flophouse hotels are upgraded into housing that gives street people a chance to get themselves back into society. The Golden West Hotel, once the filthy Broadmoor, has been restored not only for street people but also for the mentally ill who now live in clean, bright rooms and take their medicines under supervision. They visit the gallery regularly to chat with Gertrude and the two gallery cats. The hotel is run by Central City Concern, one of several agencies in Old Town that care for the down and out.

The North Park Blocks are graced with one of Portland's most beautiful buildings. The Customs House was started in 1898 and its design called for 5,000 tons of granite for its facade. Its third floor was to house the federal courts with forty feet high ceilings and there was to be a lead lined cell for unruly prisoners. However the US District judge of the time, the Hon. Charles Bellinger, began to have grave doubts about the location of his new courts and a year before the completion of the building decided he would not move under any circumstances from Pioneer Courthouse. The Customs House was completed more modestly than originally planned but at least achieved recognition in 1968 when it was placed on both the local and national landmark registers.

Joe Maras
been with Daisy Kingdom
Since Oct 25 1985

On the next block is a humbler building that is just as distinctive in its own way. As the only business for some time in a questionable neighborhood, the owners of Daisy Kingdom, a mecca for anyone who sews, made the building a beacon of cheerful design. Flags, painted flowers and bright window displays tempted suburbanites to brave the area and shop there. Joe was hired as guard and escort and, though today there is little harassment from panhandlers and drug dealers, he has become a permanent fixture of the Park Blocks. He is the local tour guide, raconteur and informant on every subject.

Another welcome addition to the Pearl District has been the advent of the microbreweries. In 1984, thanks to the lobbying efforts of a group of ardent beer lovers, the law in Oregon was changed to allow beer to be brewed and drunk on the same premises, providing the number of gallons produced annually did not exceed 10,000, a number that has escalated upwards to 200,000 today. BridgePort was the first to open, quickly followed by Widmer and Portland Brewing. Beer tourists are a new breed and there are few more pleasant ways to spend a summer evening than quaffing a pint or

Bridge Port Brew Pub.
1313 N.W. Marshall.
Portland Ore 1989

two on the loading dock of the BridgePort Brew Pub or on the sidewalk in front of Portland Brewing. Portland can now be rightfully called the microbrewing capital of this country. Once one has sampled BridgePort's Coho Pacific or Portland Brewing's McTarnahan prizewinning ale, it is impossible to return to a Bud or a Miller Lite no matter how alluring their advertisements!

The Armory

Coyote Chandler.

from Joplin Missouri
ex Cowboy — Bronc Rider
Freight train brought me here.
Got to be in good shape to ride
them freight trains.

The Armory on NW 11th also houses beer. It is a warehouse for the Blitz Weinhard Brewing Company, but it has a more glorious history than just as a warehouse. The oldest armory in Oregon, it was built in 1889 for a cost of $40,000 and provided lodging for 250 soldiers, two Gatling guns and one brass cannon. Henry Corbett, during the opening ceremonies, called the building a "substantial and noble structure". Times changed and during the closing ceremonies in the 1950's, General George White likened it to a cowbarn that was a disgrace to the city, to the state and to the federal government. He subsequently had to apologize to the dairy industry for the comparison.

Before leaving the Pearl District, I should mention that with gentrification have come innumerable galleries, trendy furniture shops and antique malls. The First Thursday Gallery Walk has become the "in" event at which to be seen, and crowds throng Glisan Street eyeing each other more, I suspect, than the art. However the area still maintains a balance. The auto part stores are still here, as are the office furniture and electrical fixture warehouses, printing houses and Fullers, bastion of the true American breakfast. Many of the artists have fled to the inner eastside in search of cheaper rents but one hopes that the industrial nature that has been the backbone of the area will never disappear completely.

David · Javir · Lobo · Spotted Elk · James Kills on top · George little wolf · flavio C.

OLD TOWN

Old Town has always had a bawdy reputation. Thanks to its location near the port there have been saloons, nightclubs and flophouses and in earlier times, opium dens and gambling joints. A few years ago it seemed as though it was going to lose an ever escalating battle with aggressively drunk panhandlers and worse, with blatant drug dealing. The Historic Old Town Association, a group of the area's business owners, decided to tackle the problem head on. They lobbied the City for a precinct on NW Third, an area so bad that the corner of Couch was called "Death Valley". The "Cop Shop" opened in 1991, the foot, bicycle and horse patrols increased and an "exclusion" zone was put into force. Any previously booked or jailed drug dealer who was found dealing again was banned from Old Town. Fortified wine was also banned, the SRO program picked up and now Old Town appears to be winning the battle. Not that drug dealing has vanished. Other neighborhoods in Portland report a marked increase in vagrants, but Old Town has become a destination and the thrust is now to make it the nightclub and entertainment center of Portland. A controversy rages at the moment over Erickson's Saloon on NW Second Avenue. One of Portland's most famed drinking holes, it claimed to have the longest bar, six hundred feet of polished wood, in the world. The building was bought and restored by the Naito family and until now housed

George J. Pappas

Linda & Mike
from the Gas Board

Anastasia CORIS

the only museum in this country dedicated to advertising. The museum will move across the river to the newly restored Metro building and Erickson's Saloon will return to its original purpose, a drinking and nude dancing establishment. Anastasia, owner of Johnny's Greek Villa on NW Third, hopes the saloon will open. It will bring increased business not only to the restaurant but also to the Greek nightclub, complete with bouzoukia and belly dancing, that she plans to open. Johnny's has always been our favorite haunt for Greek taverna food. It was previously owned by the Pappas brothers, George and Bill, who sold it to Anastasia a couple of years ago. She is from the same village in the Peloponnese that they are, and George is frequently to be found cooking in the kitchen. I suppose once a restaurateur it is hard to give up! Usually though, it is Anastasia and her two daughters, Eleni and Vicki, who man the kitchen and the tables.

Next door is Darcelle XV. Walter, aka Darcelle, has owned the club for so long, 27 years, that it has become a Portland institution. He attributes the club's success to the fact that the show has emphasized the burlesque tradition of female impersonators. I feel that another reason for its success is the amount of time that Walter, as Darcelle, has donated to the community. He has served on innumerable committees, the most recent the Lighting Committee for Old Town, and appeared for free at fund raisers of every kind though recently his emphasis has shifted to any event that is Aids related. It was with fascination that we watched a somewhat plump middle aged man transform himself into Darcelle over a period of an hour. Walter has two grandchildren and I asked if they knew what he did for a living. "Good Heavens no!" was his reply, "but the oldest is wondering why there are so many photographs of an ugly over madeup lady in my apartment!" Equally fascinating was to see a pleasant looking boy in a back to front baseball cap change himself into a spectacularly beautiful female. I learned a lot about makeup techniques! The show is hilarious, somewhat risqué but never offensive. Darcelle and Co. had their audience of mostly young females rocking in the aisles. The club is obviously a popular place for a girls' night out!

Eleni
of
"Johnny's"

Darcelle

The Chinese Gate

CHINESE GATEWAY

To the west of NW Second is Chinatown. The original Chinatown was located on the other side of Burnside and the community at the turn of the century numbered 7,800. Many were refugees from Seattle and Tacoma where the Chinese were considerably worse treated than in Portland. The Chinatown Gateway on NW Fourth was constructed in Taiwan and shipped to Portland in four containers. In October 1986, Yu Tang Wang, its designer, arrived and spent a feverish week working day and night to reassemble it in time for the opening ceremonies. It was officially dedicated at the beginning of November with speeches, dragon dances and firecrackers and now stands as an entrance to Chinatown and a symbolic gateway to increased friendship, trade and goodwill to Pacific Rim countries. There is also a sneaking satisfaction in knowing that the bronze lions at the base, unlike San Francisco's, are correctly placed. The male symbolizing "Yang" is on the left, and the female, "Yin", is on the right.

SW THIRD AVENUE

There is a block on SW Third between Oak and Stark that houses several diverse businesses. There is the Portland Outdoor Store which has sold tack and Western apparel for the past seventy years on the same site. It has been in the hands of the Popick family since the 1930's and today is run by Lynda, Brad and Diane, grandchildren of the store's founder. Next door is the Red Sea restaurant and dance club which is, I'm told, one of the best places to dance in Portland. Bwana Junction has been on the block for more than thirty years. It is owned by Joseph Lai, a member of the Middle Kingdom, so he says, who arrived in Portland as a child. His father owned a store in Chinatown and Joseph vividly remembers the Depression; one working light bulb in the family's apartment and dinners of a bowl of rice with an egg in it. He says there was overt discrimination during those years and he caused a number of

9 pens?!

Lea's Office

Anna Marie & Joseph Lae

49

eyebrows to be raised when he married Anna Marie; mixed marriages forty years ago were unheard of. But, he says they have achieved perfect balance, the yin and the yang of children, two boys and two girls! Joseph sells rifles, pistols, fishing rods and paraphernalia for hunters. On the southern corner of the block is Cameron's Bookstore, a chaos of old magazines, comics and secondhand books.

Cameron's sits on the site of the first Roman Catholic cathedral in Portland. A year later, in 1879, a house designed by Prosper Heurn was built next door to house Archbishop Blanchet. The cathedral was moved to Northwest Portland in 1890, but the ornately Gothic Bishop's House (wrongly named) still stands. One of its main features was a musicians' gallery from which the Archbishop would entertain his guests with sacred music sung by the cathedral's choir. Times changed and by the 1930's, the archbishop's balcony held the band that entertained the customers of the speakeasy that operated below. Later on, during a major refit, wires were discovered that ran from the Bishop's House to the police station behind it. One wonders who was bugging whom! Other tenants have included a Chinese Tong, the American Institute of Architects and various restaurants. Gus Haddad's Al Amir Lebanese Restaurant has been in the Bishop's House for four years now and serves, if his publicity is to be believed, food fit for princes and maybe for archbishops too!

Adnan and Gus Owners of the AL-AMIR Restaurant

Street Side Merchants are popping up all over Portland. — you can buy anything! from chicken to Indian Jewellery.

51

The Dekum Building

Further south along Third Avenue is the massive Dekum Building. It was built in 1893 entirely of materials found in Oregon, and is one of the few surviving examples of the Richardsonian-Romanesque style in Portland. Frank Dekum was born in Bavaria, arrived in Portland in 1852 and immediately opened Portland's first bakery. His real passion was for songbirds and, through his presidency of the German Songbird Society, he introduced nightingales, goldfinches and starlings to Oregon. I am not sure why he thought starlings so exotic. Each spring, as they build their noisy nests in the eaves of our house, I'm inclined not to think too kindly of Mr. Dekum! His building is another Portland landmark that has been restored by the Naito family and, being an innovator, I am sure he would appreciate the renovations to the fourth floor. A baseball court complete with bleachers and scoreboard has been constructed there for the staff of the advertising agency of Wieden and Kennedy.

A block to the east is Huber's Restaurant, the oldest in Portland. It started life as the Bureau but the name changed to Huber's in 1895. In 1888 Frank Huber, by then sole owner, hired a young Chinese immigrant, Jim Louie from Canton, to help with the making of the turkey sandwiches for which the saloon was famous. There is a story of the young Jim, during the flood of 1894, serving sandwiches and clams from a boat behind the bar while the saloon's patrons rowed across to pick them up. Huber's moved to its present location in 1911. Frank Huber died and Jim took over as bartender. The place nearly closed during Prohibition but, at the urging of the many regulars, it was turned into a restaurant for a cost of forty dollars. Jim Louie worked there every day until his death when his half share passed to his nephew, Andrew. The Louie family finally bought out the Hubers and today the restaurant is run by Andrew's children, James, David and Lucille. The decor has hardly changed since 1911. The wood panelling and stained glass skylight, even the brass cash register, are all original. Roast turkey is still on the menu and Spanish coffee, served with great flair, is still the most popular item.

53

CITY HALL

City Hall is almost dwarfed by the PacWest Tower and Michael Graves' Portland Building but its three stories provides a sense of scale to their massiveness. Designed in the Italianate palazzo style by William Whidden a hundred years ago, it will soon have to undergo major repair to bring it up to the new earthquake codes. The main entrance will once more face 4th Avenue and the restoration will return both the interior and exterior to their former beauty.

Portland's first mayor was Hugh O'Bryant who was elected by one vote in 1851, the year the city was incorporated but the city's most colorful mayor was George L. Baker. Elected in 1917, he started his career as a cleaner of monkey cages at Cordray's Theater but soon became a showman and owner of a vaudeville troupe and a number of downtown theaters. He was called "the champion loud noise of the Pacific Northwest," and was an unashamed booster of industry and everything American. Trade Unions, and in particular the Wobblies, the Industrial Workers of the World, were anathema to him and he never hesitated to use his police force to put down strikes. In 1922, a hundred special police brutally stopped a strike on Portland's waterfront and George Baker took credit for averting a revolution. It must have been the right formula as he remained in office for seventeen years.

Bud Clark would probably qualify as a colorful Portland mayor. A tavern owner and complete underdog, Bud defeated the Establishment's man, Frank Ivancie, in the primary of 1984. We saw him for the first time on a bathroom door in Athens many years ago. His poster "Expose Yourself to Art" had achieved world fame, possibly aided by the prurient thought that maybe Bud was wearing nothing under the raincoat, though he has assured us he was. After his election he appeared on the Johnny Carson and other national TV shows and

The City Hall. Portland. Papas 1993.

Vera Katz

suddenly our East Coast friends knew where we lived. Portland was that faraway city where the mayor exposed himself to art and barked; Bud's "Whoop, whoop" echoed far afield! Bud is proud that he has presided over eight years of such remarkable growth and change to the city.

Vera Katz, his successor, does not think that the next ten years will see as much change as there is less public money available for big projects. The focus, she feels, will be on the new River District to the north and the expansion of offices and apartments to the south of RiverPlace. We met Vera early one morning before she participated in the Mayor's Forum, a weekly live cable program. She has been in politics a long time and is remembered in the State Legislature as the only person who served three terms as Speaker of the House. It took 101 ballots to get her elected the first time. "I had several strikes against me," she said. "I was Jewish, a woman and I was pro sales tax!" Her new job, she says, is entirely different. It is more managerial and she gets impatient with small, local issues. She does not, she says, particularly enjoy sitting through a two hour debate on whether to cut down a city tree or not. But the plus side is to be part of major issues such as how best to tackle Portland's expansion over the next twenty years. As we leave she is cussing out the new sound system which is far too loud. Vera radiates high energy and perhaps more importantly, a good sense of humor.

TRANSIT MALLS

The transit malls on Fifth and Sixth Avenues extend all the way across Burnside to Union Station and the Greyhound Bus Station. All buses that run along the malls and around downtown are part of Fareless Square. As the name implies, the rides are free, a fact that always astonishes first time visitors to the city. The transit malls also provide a showcase for some of Portland's outdoor sculpture. Without doubt, Portlandia is the most

important statue, if only by virtue of size. She was ensconced above the Fifth Avenue entrance of the Portland Building with much fanfare in 1986. The second largest hammered copper statue in the USA, (the Statue of Liberty is the largest) she made her way to Portland from the East Coast via train, a barge upriver and finally flatbed truck. The final stages of her journey were witnessed by thousands of people.

Jerry
Hulsman.

The University Club
Portland.
Pepas 1993

Some of the city's most impressive architecture is also showcased on the malls. The Portland Building has been one of the city's most controversial buildings. Designed by Michael Graves, it was the first major Post-Modern building in the country and while the exterior is certainly eye-catching, the dark and depressingly colored interior has been likened to a public lavatory. Less controversial is the Hugh Stubbin's designed PacWest Center with its horizontal bands of glowing aluminum. The recently built Pioneer Tower is part of Pioneer Place, the highly successful downtown mall. Jerry

Hulsman's offices are here. He grew up on a farm in Cornelius, spent fifteen years in Washington DC, returned to Portland in 1979 and started a brokerage business. Jerry is proud of the city. He feels downtown is very viable and in some ways like Europe with its vitality and diversity. It is a good place to do business too. Oregon at the moment is first or second in growth in the nation because, he says, it never fell to pieces. There were no big ups and downs so momentum kept going. Looking at Portland from his office, I can see the river and mountains and feel appreciation for the planners who have been so instrumental in maintaining Portland's beauty. The city blocks were designed to be smaller than is usual so there is appreciably more light and space between buildings.

Clubs have played an important role in the formation of Portland's power structure. The Arlington, opened in 1867, was for the business and social elite to discuss "their own and Portland's destiny". Only recently, after a lengthy battle, have women been admitted through its doors. The University Club was a little more democratic. Its qualification for membership in 1898, the year it was founded, was a college degree and sufficent funds to pay the initiation fee of $5 and the monthly dues of $1. The Club is housed in a classic brick building that has changed little since the time it was built.

The *Oregonian* has played as important a part in shaping Portland's ideas and ideals as have the clubs. The paper has been part of the city since 1850 when it started life under the editorship of Thomas Dryer. Mr. Dryer was a man of strong views which he did not hesitate to voice. His comments about *Salem's Statesman* were typical, "a complete tissue of gross profanity, obscenity, falsehood and meaness" was how he wrote about his rival. Henry Pittock, who had started as a printer, bought the paper in 1860 and remained as publisher well into the 20th century. He hired Harvey Scott who, as editor for forty years, did much to keep the *Oregonian* in the front rank of American newspapers.

Bill Hilliard has also had a major role in keeping the *Oregonian* in the forefront. He retired this summer but during his forty two years with the paper, twelve of which were as editor in charge, he presided over many changes. Bill was born in Arkansas but came to Portland with his mother in 1936. He says it was the best thing that ever happened to him and describes his surprise, as a young black boy, to find himself in a racially integrated school. He started his first newspaper at the age of nine and soon graduated to producing, writing and editing the Benson High School tabloid. After a job as a redcap at Union Station he started as copy boy on the *Oregonian* in 1952. His big break came during a union walkout seven years later. He broke the picket line, was hired as a reporter, became city editor in 1972 and editor in chief ten years later. He reckons he was probably the only black reporter on the west coast writing major

The Performing
Art Center with
Bob, Kiffi, Timi,
Steve, Mike,
Zea, Peta, Aroon
Aziz & Vollmer,
passing bye.

stories for a major newspaper during the 1960's. He recalls covering an NAACP meeting for the *Oregonian*. Franklin Williams, the president, asked him what paper he was from and what was the circulation. On hearing over 300,000, Mr. Williams commented that the *Oregonian* had to be the largest colored paper in the country! No major newspapers were covering such stories at that time. Bill says he has never had any desire to live anywhere other than Portland. He feels the city allows a person the freedom to express their individuality, "the experiment we call Oregon". He acknowleges there is still polarization on many issues. However, at a recent symphony concert at which he had expected to be in the minority, he was delighted to see not only whites and blacks in equal numbers, but also to realize that he hardly knew anyone. The city's health depends on such an influx of new blood, he says.

60

BROADWAY

Broadway is Portland's main thoroughfare. Every parade passes along it. The grandest hotels, the theaters, the Performing Arts Center, Pioneer Square and Nordstrom all line it. The 1920's were the high point when the exotic neon marquees of the Paramount, the Broadway and the Hippodrome attracted people downtown to attend the newly refurbished movie theaters. The Fox Theater is a survivor from earlier days. Built as the Heilig in 1910, it enjoyed the reputation as Portland's "finest legitimate theater". Quite an accolade as Portland eighty years ago had one of the best theatrical reputations in the United States. There were at least twenty theaters in the city and stars such as Madame Schumann-Heink and Walter Hampden performed regularly. Today the Fox is used for special events. It is constantly under the threat of demolition and there are fears it will suffer the same fate as the Broadway Theater with an office tower erected in its place. However, as long as the opposition to this plan keeps festering, primarily because a tall building would cast a shadow across Pioneer Square, the Fox's marquee will remain a prominent landmark of Broadway's landscape. The fifties and sixties saw Broadway's buildings, like so many downtown, fall into disrepair. However, over the past decade the Benson and the Heathman hotels have been refurbished and the Vintage Plaza has opened. The Paramount Theater reopened as the Arlene Schnitzer Concert Hall, the Broadway Theater was pulled down and the new Broadway Building erected in its place with four cinemas at ground level instead of one. The cruisers have returned and on Saturday nights three blocks of Broadway are barred to traffic. The Labor Day weekend is without doubt the busiest. Over 200,000 attend the three day Artquake celebrations and four blocks of Broadway are lined with booths crammed with artwork and crafts.

Ed Canduro
Art Collector & Connisseur.
His sculpture by Duane Hanson
"Seated Dishwasher" is so very
realistic, It had Police, who
answered an Alarm, demand that it
stick its hands up. — A plumber
called an Ambulance — because he
thought it was Dead — And
Tessa said "Good evening" to it!

The crowning glory of Broadway's rehabilitation was the opening of the Performing Arts Center in 1987. This event was highlighted by a tightrope walk by Roland Petit from the new building to the Arlene Schnitzer Hall, home of the Oregon Symphony. Designed by Robert Oringdolph, the new building houses two theaters, one seating 900 and one more casual and smaller. Unfortunately the Center has run at a loss since opening and the city is trying to come up with some innovative funding ideas. Ultimately it will be up to the citizens to show that they care sufficiently for the cultural health of their city by attending the first rate theater that is performed at the Center.

One strong believer in the creed of giving back to one's community is Dolores Winningstad. Dolores visited us in our studio and one could not but be impressed with her warmth and humor. She and another friend of ours visiting at the same time got into a discussion about Porsches. LaVonne told of the time he was pulled over by the police. "I suppose people of color shouldn't drive Porsches," he said. "And what color should they be to drive a Porsche?!" was Dolores' retort. She and her husband, Norman,

The Fox Theatre
Broadway — Portland
Papas 1993

came from California in 1959. After a stint with Tektronix, Norman started his own high tech company, Floating Point Systems, which was enormously successful. Once her three children had completed high school, Dolores had time to become involved in different arts programs. She has been on the advisory boards of the Zoo, OMSI, the Symphony and the Ballet for a while. One of the theaters at the Performing Arts Center is named after her, but her proudest sponsorship was to underwrite OPB's Sesame Street for five years. She says she is an activist and a believer that if one is involved in something, one should be totally involved, otherwise give way to someone who can make a difference. She feels that Portland is fortunate in that there are a number of people involved in the betterment of the city. She cites the proliferation of neighborhood associations and the rise in community policing. All people want is to pass along something decent to their children. Without such people, she says, the city will die. One aspect of American life that always amazes Bill and me is the amount of time people spend volunteering and the amount of money raised for different charities and causes.

OREGON HISTORICAL CENTER

The Oregon Historical Society is one of Oregon's oldest institutions. It was founded in 1873 and has been the official recorder of Oregon's history ever since. Its new headquarters, which cover most of the block between Broadway, Park and Jefferson, was built in 1966. Here, there is a museum, a reference library in which I have spent many hours, a gift shop, galleries and a plaza that, at present, is playing host to a controversial bronze sculpture of a pioneer family. The trompe l'oeil murals by Richard Haas that adorn the new building also depict the history of the pioneers, but they have been unanimously acclaimed. The Oregon Historical Society has the reputation of being one of the finest in the USA. Unlike many such institutions, it is as concerned with the present and the future as it is with the past. It also puts out a magazine, the *Oregon Historical Quarterly*, which has been published continuously since 1900.

Ted Miller. - 92 years young.
Lives in the West Hills with
Sweet Marie. Born in
Montana on a ranch, knew
the artist Charlie Russell
as a boy. Came to Oregon
in 1932. Went into the
lumber business.
Lived in a Castle
on the Riviera
for six gorgeous
summers.

Craig Hamm. gave up discipline and pursued his own desires. He retired at an early age, after selling his Insurance Company. — becoming the Ultimate Blue collar worker. Tinkering with Ancient Rolls Royces — 280 SL's — BMW Motor bikes — and at times mending lights + fixtures for Linda, his wife, and her shop. "Naomi's Lighting"

THE LIBRARY

There has been a library in Portland since 1869. The first one was housed in a building on the corner of Stark and First. Judge Matthew Deady was the library's first president and his philosophy was summed up as follows: "All experiences teaches that what costs the people nothing does but little good". In other words, if the public used the library for free they would not appreciate it. Multnomah County took it out of private hands at the turn of the century. The present library building on SW Tenth Avenue opened in 1912. Built to a design of A.E. Doyle for a cost of $465,000, it now has to undergo extensive repairs because many of its steel reinforcing bars mysteriously ended up in a house that was being built at the same time on Vista Avenue for a prominent businessman. The library is much more than just books. There are computers, database information about local companies and organizations, an art gallery, videos, tapes, talking books and even a speaker's bureau. This is besides the magazines, newspapers, and a million and half books. Two thousand people visit daily and the staff answer over 600,000 reference questions a year. The statistics are mind boggling, but for the next couple of years Portlanders will have to forgo many of these amenities thanks to the greed of an early citizen.

GOVERNOR HOTEL

After the Lewis & Clark Fair in 1900, Portland's population jumped. This inflow started a building boom and several grand hotels were constructed at this time. One was the Seward named after its proprietor, Walter Seward. Its avant garde decorative style, in particular the sconces that resemble angular spacemen, caused much comment. The interiors were equally

decorative; the rooms were richly panelled and each bed was equipped with the height of modernity, a Sealy inner spring mattress. Over the years it degenerated into a flophouse but now, thanks to Portland's latest boom, it has been restored to its former glory and renamed the Governor. Jake's Grill has taken over the restaurant and has the same period feeling, much enhanced by the original mosaic floor that was discovered under a carpet. Bill McCormick, owner of the restaurant, told us that, at the very last moment, the design of the restaurant was completely changed to accommodate the mosaics.

LIGHT RAIL

In 1906 the Portland Railway Light and Power Company operated 161 miles of railway in the Portland area. By 1910 its trains and streetcars carried over sixteen million people a year and one could travel easily from Gresham to Hillsboro and south to Salem. With the advent of the automobile, these lines were ripped up and the railways bought by the petroleum and rubber companies to ensure that nothing would compete with their sales of tires and gas. It is interesting to surmise how much Tri Met could have saved if those streetcar lines had remained! Be that as it may, and despite opposition from the media and the public, MAX started running between Gresham and downtown in September 1986. 200,000 people crowded aboard for the initial free ride and since then the numbers have averaged 20,000 riders each weekday. Today the streets west of the Morrison Street turnaround are torn up as the new westside line is installed. Next year, once again, Portlanders will be able to ride from Gresham to Hillsboro by light rail.

The Oregon Historical Society
South Park Blocks
Papas 1993.

SOUTH PARK BLOCKS

One of the first successes of Portland's early planners was to set aside twenty five city blocks for the creation of a park that would run from the hills at the south end of the city to the river at the north end. This continuation was sabotaged in 1871 when seven of the blocks in the center of town were somehow sold to private individuals and built upon. A further depredation was in the 1970's when the Federal government built the main Post Office on NW Hoyt thus ensuring that the North Park Blocks could never reach the river. Right now they end at Glisan but there is hope that the Federal

St James
Evangelical Lutheran
Church 1890-
+ the Sixth Church
of Christ Science
on the South Park B
Papas. 7

Building's parking lot between Glisan and Hoyt will be ripped up and a final park installed in the not too distant future. The South Park Blocks are more formal. There are sculptures of Theodore Roosevelt and Abraham Lincoln, among others, and flanking the trees, flower beds and paved paths are many of Portland's institutions. There is Pietro Belluschi's first major modernist structure, the Portland Art Institute, which made the AIA's list of the one hundred most influential buildings in USA between the years 1920 and 1940. There is the back of the Performing Arts Center and the front of the First

Congregational Church with its Venetian Tower. And of course there are the people who use the park; students from Portland State, tenants of the new brick apartments that have recently been built near the university, tourists and visitors to the cultural establishments and the ubiquitous homeless who lie on the park benches until told to move on by A.B. and Cary. They work for Portland Progress and patrol the parks on mountain bikes to make sure that there is no drinking, sleeping on park benches or skateboarding. There are thirty guides and officers who patrol the city's streets and parks. A.B. has been with Portland Progress since it was founded in 1988. Previously he had worked as a police officer in Fort Worth but did not want to go through the retraining required to join the Portland Police force. As an ex police officer he carries a gun, though has not had to use it yet, while Cary, his partner for three years, is a guide. "A.B. does the enforcing. I do the PR stuff," he says. Both feel that the concept of the guides has helped keep crime down and has also helped create a positive attitude about downtown.

A.B. and Cary

William L. Failing
Billy Failing

COUNCIL CREST
TROLLEY

WEST HILLS

Many members of the founding families still live in the West Hills overlooking the city. They belong to the same clubs as their grandfathers, still control a proportion of commerce in the city and still send their offspring back East to be educated. The founding fathers, most of whom were from New England, wanted a society that reflected their own somewhat narrow views and their children were sent East to imbibe the old standards. However new trends advanced more rapidly there than in the West and it has been to Portland's advantage to have these young people return home with fresh ideas. Bill Failing attended an East Coast university. The great great grandson of Josiah Failing, he lives in the West Hills and oversees a Kansas City classical music radio station and two magazines from his home. He is fascinated by his family's history and tells us that Josiah, one of Portland's first mayors, had three sons who continued the family business. One went into banking and became rich, the second became a scholar and had so many daughters that his house was known as the nunnery, and the third became a church deacon. "We have three branches of the family, the rich, the poor and the ultra religious!" he says with a laugh. It provides a nice sense of continuity that there is a Failing Building, a Failing Street and Failings still living in Portland.

Thanks to the first cablecar routes up Vista Avenue into the hills west of the city, new neighborhoods were created in the 1890's. Vista was the appropriate word for the new road as the views of the city, the rivers and mountains were stunning. Portland Heights was and still is a wonderful place to live. Generations of families have lived in the same neighborhood, some in the same houses, and they still shop at Stroheckers, the same grocery store that sold produce to their great grandparents. Another institution, but one that was recently pulled down to make way for a new shopping center, was Henry Thiele's at the bottom of Vista Avenue. Every night the bar and restaurant were full of the

Orville Noble (Mo) and
Elizabeth Ann Jones.
Mo was born in Portland
in 1909 - He's an
Orthopaedic Surgeon -
who, with Elizabeth, spent
many months in Afganistan
teaching young Doctors.
They also love cruising
the Mediterranean.

Jim Lane
Ex Cowboy
& New Yorker

"golden oldies" as Bill termed them, eating fresh smelt and finnan haddie. No waitress was much under seventy, nor was the clientele. We were introduced to its culinary delights by Mo and Elizabeth Jones, who along with Howard and Mary Baker, were the reason we had flown to Portland in the first place. We had met both couples in Greece while hosting them on a charter and had become such good friends that they joined us many times for different voyages around the eastern Mediterranean. We never dreamt as we boarded a plane in Chicago in February 1984 that we would end up living in Portland, indeed living in Howard and Mary's old house in the Heights. Howard and Mary are both deceased now but as we gaze out of the house's huge windows at the city below us we constantly thank all the happy coincidences that brought us here. It was through the Jones that we met Jim Lane. From a well to do New York family, he was supposed to have a career in law. However his love was for cattle ranching and he came to Oregon to follow his dream. He and Luise, his wife, bought an isolated ranch in southern Oregon where they lived for many years until Jim, having fallen off his horse one time too many, decided that the law looked more attractive at age 48 than it had when he was younger. He graduated from Lewis and Clark at age 51 and now has a successful immigration practice in Portland.

Papas
23rd Street
Portland OR
1984

NW 23rd AVENUE

The demise of Henry Thiele's and two other long-standing eating places, Roses and the Quality Pie Shop, on 23rd Avenue are synonymous with the changes that have taken place in this neighborhood in the ten years that we have lived in Portland.

Northwest Portland has always been densely populated as many of the old mansions owned by Portland's first business elite were converted into duplexes and triplexes. In the 1920's a number of apartment buildings were constructed to provide reasonably priced living close to downtown. It remained a residential area with a sprinkling of taverns, a couple of drugstores and grocery shops that led into the industrial and port section of the city. That was until Richard Singer and a couple of other young developers appeared on the scene in the early 1980s and founded the Nob Hill

Met Tom Goodwin in Greece in 1974. He worked on our 60ft Yacht — And always talked of Mystical — Romantic Oregon — His home! We now own a fishing boat together — it's 16ft. ___ in Oregon!

75

"Fairmont" — Monty for short.!
Companion to Jane Dillon
weight - 10½ lbs, Height - 17", Length 28"
Tuna in Salt Water — favourite Dish
Great Wanderer.

business group. They slowly bought up several of the dilapidated walk-up Victorians that lined 23rd Avenue and renovated them. The old laundromat on Everett and 23rd where Bill learned to play the Pacman video game was transformed into a charcuterie, wine and grocery shop. The espresso craze hit Portland and overnight it seemed ten places opened on 23rd to assuage the city's caffeine addiction. One of the latest, Torrefazione, is a traditional Italian (actually Perugian) coffee house with umber walls, ceramic cups, latte, espresso, and cappuccino only, no fancy almond mocca double skinnies here. Boutiques selling trendy clothes and trendy gewgaws open and close with monotonous regularity but it makes for interesting window shopping and indeed crowd watching. On weekends the street is jammed with automobiles fighting to park and with pedestrians fighting to get a vantage point at one of the sidewalk tables. Saturday afternoon is a great time to sit on a corner nursing a latte and meeting friends and watching the passing parade.

STAN HELLMAN
ex South African
ex lawyer
ex playboy.

NW 21st AVENUE

21st Avenue has been slower to change than 23rd but now it is gaining a reputation as restaurant row. Several storefronts have been transformed into some of Portland's best restaurants. The prophylactic store on the corner of NW Johnson has changed into an upscale food market and even the old Cinema 21 has been spruced up. One place that has not changed is the Nob Hill Drugstore. It gained fame as the location for Gus Van Sant's movie, *Drugstore Cowboy*, chosen because it still retained a 1950's ambience. Opposite the drugstore is the Blue Moon Tavern. In the 1970's this place achieved the dubious distinction of being the downtown hangout of the biker crowd. Pool and beer were the big attractions and apparently fights were common most Friday and Saturday nights. Today it is one of the many pubs owned by the McMenamin brothers. The pool tables are gone and it is advertised as "a neighborhood place for family and friends" which seems a little tame when compared to its biker days!

Alaska (Gallery Cat)
Sociable Rat Catcher, who
loves first Thursdays — Stands
no nonsense from Cat - Dog
or Human!

BURNSIDE

In 1912 Mr. Bennett, an English graduate of the Beaux Arts School, was asked by the city fathers to come up with a Greater Portland Plan. His design was for a city of two million with broad avenues, parks, a public waterfront area and an expanded system of roads to ease, what was a problem even then, traffic congestion downtown. There is a fascinating drawing that shows Burnside as a wide boulevard with four lines of trees, intersecting the Park Blocks on a diagonal. Portland might have ended up with an American version of the Champs Elysées! Unfortunately Mr. Bennett's plan was not approved and Burnside's main claim to fame is that it is Portland's longest street and provides the division between the north and south parts of the city. With the advent of the automobile it became car dealers' row. One building that had nothing to do with automobiles was the Crystal Ballroom. It was designed for Mr. Ringler's Dance Academy and his Cotillion Ballroom and was an instant success. This was partly due to the 7,500 square-foot dance floor, which could be adjusted by an intricate system of rockers and bearings to different types of dance rhythms and load. Through the years big names like Glenn Miller and Artie Shaw played there and later it was Jefferson Airplane and

the Grateful Dead that packed them in. By 1968, on the grounds of safety, the City Council closed the doors for good and the old ballroom stands forlornly on the corner of 14th and Burnside.

Further east on Burnside is the distinctive flatiron shape of the KKEY Building. It was built as a showroom and offices for Peerless Tire and Rubber Co. At that time it claimed to be the smallest office building in Portland and also one of the most modern; there were bathrooms on all three floors. A succession of tire companies occupied it until the KKEY radio station group moved in about 20 years' ago. Until recently their eclectic mix of jazz, religion and talk was broadcast from its 1,000 square feet.

JAKE'S FAMOUS CRAWFISH

Both Blitz Weinhard Brewing & Jake's Famous Crawfish have been around Portland for a long time. Blitz has the distinction of being the oldest continuous running brewery west of the Mississippi. Since 1876 it has been in the same location on Burnside and brews some two million barrels of beer a year. One block south is Jake's, the flagship of the McCormick and Schmick empire. Bill McCormick operates from a sprawling office in the Morgan Building. His secretary was out the day we visited so he fetched the coffee himself apologizing for the lack of elegance in the service. An ironic comment, as later in our conversation he stressed how service and commitment to the company were two cornerstones of his success. Bill was born in Rhode Island, moved to San Francisco and to an office job in 1963. He shared an apartment with a group of friends and before long, they decided that rather than constantly paying for beer it would be better to buy the local bar. One thing led to another and soon the bar had grown into a chain of successful steak houses called the Refectory. A large company bought out the chain but did not wish to include Jake's in the package, so Bill ended up in Portland with one very antiquated restaurant. "The kitchen was in the basement and all the food was hauled up by dumb waiter," he says shaking his head. However, the basement kitchen had been experimenting with fish on the menu and in the 1970's this proved a visionary idea. Bill took on a new partner, Doug Schmick. Jake's was upgraded into its present successful self and the McCormick and Schmick seafood chain has not looked back. They own fifteen restaurants on the West Coast and there are plans to open two to three new restaurants a year in the foreseeable future. The secret of his success, Bill says, has been to instill a sense of corporate pride in his employees. They also have to be willing to learn as the menu changes every day. There might be a hundred different items, most of them fish, as well as a very lengthy wine list. "I can have three different types of salmon on the menu on any given day and the waiters must know the difference between each type." He laughs as he recalls ordering salmon at a rival seafood restaurant in San Francisco and on asking where it was from, was told from the ocean! He's headquartered here for the simple reason he loves the city. "Its an easy place to live!"

Bill McCormick's wife Gail is a marathon Runner and has attempted to swim the English Channel — She almost made it! But in the last few hours the tide was against her. Better luck next time Gail!!

Michael Powell
Whose bark is much.
much worse than
his bite !!

POWELL'S

Apparently where the Oregon Trail divided there were two signs; one showed a heap of gold quartz to indicate California and the other simply read, "To Oregon". The literate came to Portland and the book business has never looked back. Powell's is the behemoth of the more than thirty independent booksellers in the city. Housed in what was an American Motors dealership on Burnside, Powell's takes up the entire block and with its recent second floor addition, lays claim to being the biggest bookstore in the country. The main store houses over 1,000,000 volumes, many of them secondhand. It can be said that if some obscure title cannot be found in Powell's one can be fairly confident that it cannot be found anywhere else in the country. It is more than just a bookstore however. The Ann Hughes coffeeshop acts as a de facto library; a place where one can take a book off the shelf, read it over a cup of latte, and return it. Authors put in guest appearances to read and autograph their latest books, and, thanks to the store being open 365 days a year from 9 am until 11 pm, it is one of the city's most popular meeting places. Michael Powell's father started the bookstore in 1971. Michael, though born in Portland, spent many years in Chicago before returning to take over from his father in 1980. A few years ago we had asked him his opinion about the chances of a book on Portland selling well. His answer had been very discouraging!

Nathan

SKATEBOARDERS' PARK

Under the Burnside Bridge on the east side is a bowl shaped area that looks as though the craziest of graffiti artists has had several nightmares. We were enlightened by Nathan, a sixteen year old from Vancouver, who was resting on his skateboard. Skateboarders, he says, are discriminated against in the city. There are city ordinances that forbid skateboarding in the parks, and there is controversy as to whether skateboards should be allowed on sidewalks or whether they are a vehicle and should keep to the streets. So, a group of kids decided to create their own skateboard park. Over four years ago the group approached Bud Clark and obtained permission from the City to build it. Some company lent a Caterpillar to dig the holes and create the hammocks and hillocks but otherwise twenty boys built the park entirely by themselves. Actually, it is still not finished as the boys constantly modify and change the landscape to make the skating more exciting. Sloan joined the conversation. At any time there might be a hundred boys skating, he said. They come from all over the city to skate after school and at weekends. Have they had any trouble from gangs, we asked. Sloan laughed and said the skateboarders would take care of any gang member if they tried anything! We hadn't realized that skateboarding is almost a religion, with its own language, with devotees from eight year olds to young men well into their twenties, and of course with its uniform of baggy pants and sneakers. And the wall paintings? They were done, Nathan told us, by a graffiti artist named Manic!

The near east side, for so long the poor relative of westside Portland, is coming into its own. Lloyd Center has been revamped, the twin green towers of the new Convention Center have became part of the city's skyline and the new Blazer Arena will soon add to it. The Blazers evoke a lot of emotion in this town. We knew nothing about basketball when we arrived, but the first time we had an inkling that the game was important was when we were asked in a New York grocery store where we were living. On hearing Portland, the response was, "Oh yes, the home of the Blazers!" Gradually we were initiated into the technicalities of the game, but it was not until the Blazers played in the finals against Chicago that we became fully indoctrinated. Our guide was George, the then cook at Johnny's Greek Villa. During the playoffs it was difficult to get a timely meal and that year it was impossible to get anything at all during the finals. George was a total addict and he would leap about the restaurant's little bar exhorting the Blazers to "sooot!" and to "thos tou ena!" (give them one). And we found that we were becoming just as addicted. Now we dread the playoffs as it means sleepless nights when the Blazers lose, miserable next morning dissections of what could have happened if only so and so had got that basket, or so and so else hadn't fouled, and of course euphoria when a game is won. Obviously, the next step will have to be season tickets at the new Rose Garden Arena!

Skaters beneath the Burnside Bridge.

White Eagle Tavern on Russell Street Has the Oldest Continuous Liquor License in Portland.

HOLLYWOOD THEATER

One thrust of the city has been to restore the old neighborhoods, in effect recreating the little towns that existed at the turn of the century before they were swallowed up into Greater Portland. An early example of this trend is the Hollywood District near NE Broadway and Sandy Boulevard which has been a viable neighborhood since the 1920's. The crown jewel of the neighborhood has to be the Hollywood Theater. "This palace of luxury, comfort and entertainment, unsurpassed by any theater on the coast" opened its doors in 1926 with much fanfare, admission cost 25¢ and the first movie shown was called "More Work - Less Pay", which sounds familiar! Hollywood was also the site of the first Fred Meyer "One stop Shopping" Center. In 1931, it was a novel idea to be able to buy food, tobacco, clothes, to have shoes mended and to eat in a restaurant under one roof. Other innovative ideas included self service, shopping baskets on wheels, the forerunner of the ubiquitous shopping cart and free parking. The Fred Meyer stores were started by Frederick Grubmeyer who was born in Brooklyn, came west to the Alaskan gold fields and finally opened a coffee and tea store on 1st and Washington with very little capital. Fred had changed his name before

86

arriving in Portland and, at the time of his death in 1978, Fred Meyer Inc. was doing over a billion dollars worth of business a year. He had amassed a personal fortune of $125 million, most of which was left to a charitable trust that plays a big part in under-writing many different charities and causes today.

BAGDAD THEATER

Another neighborhood that has undergone a renaissance is the SE Hawthorne Boulevard area around 38th Avenue. Boutiques, coffeeshops, a Powells bookstore line the street and it too is anchored by an old movie theater. The Bagdad was one of a string of exotically named theaters built in many of east Portland's neighborhoods during the 1920's. The Egyptian, the Orpheum, the Oriental and the Bagdad strove to outdo each other in rococo decor. The Oriental, which was on Grand Avenue, seated 2,000 people and its foyer was a recreation of the temple of Angkor Wat. The Bagdad was not so flamboyant. Its architecture was merely a mixture of Moorish and Mediterranean while its foyer walls featured stencilled real and mythological animals. However, the Bagdad is the sole survivor of the old eastside movie houses and, as it is now on the National Register of Historical Buildings, is here to stay.

89

U.S.S. Blue Back Submarine
on the Willamette —
In front of OMSI.

OMSI

The new OMSI, the Oregon Museum of Science and Industry, opened last year on the site of an old steam driven power plant, part of which has been incorporated into the architecture of the new museum. The red smoke stack, glass tower, copper domed Omnimax theater and the black hull of the newly donated submarine add up to a distinctive landmark on the east bank of the Willamette. Marilynne Eichinger, the director, is the force behind what is regarded as one of the most innovative science museums in the country. She is a small woman who, even after a debilitating week of conferences and late nights, exudes energy. She is from Michigan and has a background in psychology. She realized early on that she wanted to create a science museum where children could learn from interacting with a scientific exhibit rather than just by pushing a button or by merely observing. She feels strongly that people need to be trained to think and to learn how to be flexible, particularly in a future that seems increasingly insecure. And what better way than to get the school systems involved so that as many children as possible can be given access to the hands on exhibitions. She started her first museum in her basement and had graduated to a 50,000 square foot space before being asked to head OMSI in 1985. Portland, she said with a grin, was the only city that she and her husband could agree upon as a place they would both like to live. She was very involved in the design of the museum and emphasized that she wanted a space with friendly dimensions, not one that intimidated or one where parents might worry about losing their offspring. Another area in which she has been extremely innovative is in developing travelling exhibitions. OMSI at present has as many on the road as the Smithsonian, twenty four in number, and soon will have exhibitions in Europe and Australia as well. Marilynne emphasizes the benefits of these exhibitions. A great deal of publicity is generated for Portland. Other museums buy the different components of the exhibits so work is generated for small businesses here and, by collaborating with other organizations, corporate sponsorship is much easier to obtain. We leave excited that Portland has the good fortune to have such a dynamo running one of its most important showcases.

91

CORNO'S

As one drives down MLK Boulevard, without doubt the brightest objects to catch one's eye are the oversized fruit and vegetables on the now defunct Corno's Food Market. At the turn of the century a young Calabrian named Jim Corno started to sell vegetables door to door. He was so successful that his business expanded to a stall in the Yamhill Market and later to the Corno's Food Market. Sadly, the family went out of business a few years' ago and the building was recently sold. One hopes that the new owner will keep the vegetables on the roof as they have become a distinctive feature of the neighborhood.

PIONEER COURTHOUSE SQUARE

It seems appropriate to finish this personal and somewhat idiosyncratic look at Portland with Pioneer Courthouse Square. The first schoolhouse was built here in 1856, but thirty years' later it was demolished to make way for the Portland Hotel, one of Henry Villard's grandiose dreams. He went broke before the building was completed and for a while, it and Union Station, another of his grand designs, were known as Villard's ruins. However both were completed a few years later with, it was noted with pride, local money. The huge hotel became the gathering place of Portland's socially elite until 1950, when it was torn down to make way for a parking lot. It was the controversy surrounding the plan to build an eleven story parking garage in the late 1960's that galvanized the city into action. A nationally juried competition was won by Will Martin and his team and, after a cost of over $8 million, the square opened in 1984. The older generation still decried the loss of the old hotel and the wasted space of an open square

but without doubt it is a great success. It has become the city's focal point, its "living room" as Will Martin called it. For us it symbolizes the changes we have witnessed over our ten year residence here. Not only in appearance has Portland changed, but it has progressed from Tom McCall's much quoted "Come to Oregon but don't stay" attitude to one that welcomes newcomers. They are the ones who are bringing new life, new ideas, new cultures, and new tolerances to the city. Yan Borodovsky is a case in point. He and his wife Natasha, were thrown out of the Soviet Union in the 1970's because of their dissident views. Natasha, in particular, was deemed "too politically active". They arrived in California with $270, no English and one introduction. Yan, a nuclear physicist with papers published in this country, soon started work with NASA, but after seven years he and Natasha tired of California. Someone suggested they should look at Oregon so they came, fell in love with Portland and never left. Today Yan is a scientist with Intel, Natasha has a house with a wonderful garden and what was Kiev's loss has certainly been this city's gain.

Bud Clark introduced this book with the Skidmore Fountain quotation about good citizens. From the earliest pioneers to the latest influx, Portland has been fortunate with the people who have chosen to live here. It is a city that encourages individualism; Oregon, for instance, has more small businesses per capita than any other state. People move here not to make a fortune but to enjoy, in the words of that overused phrase, "the quality of life". Its a great place to live and even with 500,000 new citizens expected over the next decade, it can expect, thanks to the farsightedness of its planners, to continue to be America's "most livable city".

Yan Borodovsky

Papas 1993. *Pioneer Square Portland*

94

Oisin McCutcheon
Artist a great
Irish Story teller
and his mentor   Charlie Reynolds
/ Musician & Painter/

DIGGER O'DELLS
OYSTER BAR & RESTAURANT
OYSTERS LUNCH
HALF SEA
SHELL FOOD

STARK
NEXT SIGNAL

GRAND

U.S.
BANK

Papas
1990

CICLO
ONE WAY

FOOD
BEVERAGES

RC

Mind it
Freddys

PREPARE TO
JESUS

BICYCLE
REPAIRS

INN COUCH

Papas.

ALMA LAWRENZ

chanteuse'
a Cabaret Singer.